At the Point

At the Point

Joseph Massey

Shearsman Books

2011

First published in the United Kingdom by
Shearsman Books Ltd.,
58 Velwell Road,
Exeter
EX4 4LD

www.shearsman.com

ISBN 978-1-84861-166-5

Design and Composition by Yuki Kites.

to Humboldt County

of this:
sight's fire
furled; a

sea
channelling
inwards

—Karin Lessing

Contents

The Process

Cross-stitched
outside sounds
double the day's

indoor confusion.
How to untwine
noise, to see.

There's the bay,
highway slashed
beneath; water

a weaker shade
of gray than this
momentary sky's

widening bruise.
The page turns
on the table, bare

despite all
I thought was
written there.

¤

The Lack Of

for Pam Rehm

i.

Sunset's requisite sparrows
clamor in the shrubbery.
How the room falls, falls

further into formlessness,
around itself,
and memory—

cast to the moon's
glassed transmissions.

ii.

Where I feel my mouth
might be,
a wordlessness

mums.
The tremble
my hands trace.

Shadows
that quaver

and carve
the room.

iii.

Woke to white
windows,
whether dusk

or dawn
I didn't
know. Even

as debris
signaled
a night

spent. Pages
and pages
mistaken for months.

iv.

Is there a voice today
to write in,
beyond

what I alone
mumble?

These words
plunged daily
into hunger.

v.

On staple-pocked telephone poles
expired fliers flag. Over-
lapping lines
of obstructed light

hold the wall.
A rattle
of leaves.

vi.

Afternoon—this morning's haze
still holds, italicizing hills
that seem to float
over the highway, the horizon.

vii.

Just enough
sun nudged

past low
clouds
to uncover

an entire
sequence
of hills,

each edge
and angle.

viii.

Around traffic
and buildings

sun bends,
burns off

morning
haze, blots

the day's
gathering

names.

ix.

Light gashed
over the bay
makes the water
appear

more like steel

than things soon to rust

in the adjacent
scrapyard.

x.

What would become a field
cracks the parking lot's
bleached asphalt.

Pissed-on nasturtiums
stretch beneath a wooden fence—

every other slat punched out—
and lurch along

a fallen wall
into black overgrowth.

xi.

October's ready-made
metaphors,
almost hidden

behind billboards
and vacant warehouses,

measure the afternoon's
accumulations—

the overcast
undertones—
this slow vacillation.

xii.

Wind turns
the page
prematurely

as cattail grass,
laced through

a chain-link fence,
wavers.

xiii.

Gnats
knot sun's
white flush

through eucalyptus
limbs; leaves
lathed

in it—black.

xiv.

Fragments
of fragments

fill the hollow
of the day.

Thoughts lost

resound in
not being found.

And the weather's
changed, again.

Rain—

recollection.

¤

Close

Hedges
dredged in
shadow, where

a song's
confusion
roosts, tell

the time.

Untitled

White sun sunk
gray as memory,

as yesterday's
errors

lose voice,
as a word

is erased
into the blank

space
that bore it.

Hibernaculum

Hail on the roof
repeats, repeats

in and out of sleep,
winter's rough

translation
of itself

and a dream's
drowsy

disassembly.
The rubble

I recover.

Geography

Walk out into morning—
the hills beyond
the houses

halved by haze so white
it takes
a blue tinge.

An egret draws its shadow
over the pavement
as my mind

moves through this field
of objects.
To keep walking—

thinking—as if a world
would be there—*here*—
in a name.

No Name Pond

Attached to blackberry thorns
a plastic bag balloons

beside a faded sign:
NO ARTIFICIAL LURES.

Insects click
in brick and wood—

a kind of metronome
my mind stumbles to.

Two Pages From a Small Winter Notebook

Prescription bottle's amber
alights on the desk, floats

there; the day thinned out
through a curtain,

its mold. How the hours
pull together, pause,

in shrubs woven
with trash and nasturtiums.

■

Moon's lucid murmur.

Skunk-laced night.

Drunk, I lean on the cold
walls of my cottage

behind hydrangeas

and piss into the rain.

After Last Night's Drinking

After last night's drinking,
thoughts refuse to puncture
layers of misremembrance.
Patternless patterns—

all that's fallen with weather—
dissociate in another gust. There
a child's chalked hieroglyphs
blend, as if to mimic

this ache around my eyes. A bird,
a blur on the horizon, takes the shape
of steam lifting from a turd
where gravel meets grass,

while the noon siren sounds its vowel.

Backdrop

From this hill's vantage
all things become
whatever wind
makes them.

Electronic church bells
peal past overlapped
crow calls—

one left
circling,
recircling
a car lot.

Alley

Doberman chained to a fence post
          barks at fog folding
off the bay.

And pigeons graze garbage
          scattered near scrap metal
rusted orange.

Dizzied by the weather's syntax
          as it swerves within
these inflected things, I

lean against the garage—
          blackberry thorns
prick my palms.

Sunday

Old news—after a storm—
torn apart between two lawns.

Found

There's little
to say. The landscape

overwhelms an impulse
to speak. Sky clouded

by cloudlessness.
Almost dusk.

A dog or a child's sound
ricochets through the park.

And the ocean's drone
drones. The impulse

is enough.

Inventory

To think thinking's
    like the landscape:
this stroboscopic
    throb of things
as they ravel
    and unravel
a bus window.

The glass becomes
    a palimpsest
of eucalyptus
    torn into a barn,
into train tracks,
    into clouds warped
into an empty mall
    parking lot.

Across the street
    a stray cat
stalks a puddle's edge
    in grass overgrown
around a closed motel.

Exit North

Exhaust shrouds
a shrub in bloom
on the corner, too
distant to discern
its color. Red
graffiti underscores
a sign that points north.
March—spring singes
the sky's organized
incisions. Plastic
drifts into hydrangeas.
The pause before
one perception
extinguishes another,
extinguishes nostalgia.
Late winter waste
clumped shallow over grates.

A Line Made by Walking

Humid June
air that barely

moves, and yet
the water in the

creek wrinkles,
pushed around

fronds and
broken bottle,

or is it
chipped quartz

trapping the
glare. Rusted

shed at the road's
shoulder falls back

into flowering
brush falling over

the hill's edge.
Train tracks, grass-

smothered, run
behind it. A crow

collects trash
from a strip-

mall parking lot,
carries it to the

church roof,
then claps off

to collect more
as a gnat—no

a floater in
my right eye

bobs back and forth.
Traffic's sustained

sibilance grows
louder later. Still

the sun's white,
the haze is

white, the air
is locked

in it, and I
squint, and lean

into it, as if
to find

a word there.

Degrees

Haze faintly
         imprinted
with buildings, hills,
         a mountain.
Off-white

      sun
drums through,
glazing the nouns,
the names.
      Line by line

the landscape's
defined
         and revised
at every
      turn.

Turned

On the path
a condiment packet's
            coagulated
yellow

prods the periphery.
My sight sinks back
            into the creek's
brackish water

stirring blackened stone
            and a paint can's
red rust.

Notice

By the parking lot
of a house
emptied after foreclosure,
a yellow-jacket

slinks
through curved rain
into a half-opened fuchsia—
both heavy with water.

Motion

Highway overpass—
tagged concrete,
trash-stitched fence—

anchors sky. White
and yellow limbs
lean in

traffic's opposite direction.

Bench

Cut grass, gasoline,
mound of rotted
weeds in a vacant lot

—the scent cast,
dense, with
each breeze—in

flustered shade.
What's in a day's
name: its slowly

summoned rhythms
looped through
the music-

less field—after-
noon's clamor:
huddled

cars, deflated
bass lines
at a red light,

an argument
rattling the blue
aluminum trailer.

Forming

The languages
we dream—

their dissolution
into morning's

striations,
what scores

the contours
of the room

we find ourselves
breathing in—

how they leave us
without speech,

in pieces—a part
of the pattern

day consumes
to become.

¤

From a Window

The shadow does not move.
—William Carlos Williams

i.

Day ascends into day,
and last night's
vocabulary
is lost.

Through the bone
of a stutter

lodged in my throat,
to somehow say
what wants to be said.

Say it.

Black moth
wrecked
against glass.

Cactus aglow
on a narrow ledge.

ii.

A bulk
of clouds

broken over
dawn—

blackbirds
disperse.

Page
as white
as the sun.

iii.

This year's
        first few
rhododendrons

        hover above
purple and orange
        flowers I

can't find
        in the field guide.

iv.

Paint can
        half-sunk
in dried mud

        full of yesterday's
               rain.

v.

Lit amber by
back door light

a skunk prowls
bramble's edge

—blackberry vines
and dandelions

bunched alongside
the garage—

into alley's black
spilling moths.

vi.

Weeds after
days of rain
and fog
curve

from one end
of the sidewalk
to the other

above snails crushed
last night
while I walked home
drunk in the dark.

vii.

In vines'

leaves
latticed over
the sunk shed roof

gnats or bees
—both—blur.

viii.

Over the window
        cobwebs
embody a breeze
        neither of us feel.

ix.

Gibbous moon
splinters

past bare
fuchsia branches

and my face
cast

on lamp-glared
glass.

x.

Dawn skims the blinds
into a shape   shadows

—children, traffic, pigeons
cut across—

          What's left of the dream:
          a hole in my head

          the dreamed words
          draw through and decompose.

xi.

The hills
aligned

with clouds
aligned

with the
windowsill

levitate.

¤

Prescription

To think through
each word's
particular weather.

To stand
just far enough
outside of the page.

A field drapes
the eye
in limitless revision.

How shadows
that fill the gap
between two stones

imply the sky's weight.

No Vehicles Beyond this Point

Tape unspools from a cassette,
          collects—a nest—between two
pieces of driftwood, measures
          the wind's direction. Wind pinched
with skunk, sea salt, gasoline.

Lull

Lethargy
of a bee

in October.
Hummingbird

hung up
in cold.

The field's
periphery

swollen
with color

gathers
what's left

of this
particular

light—

summer's
arrested

tatters.
Words

I didn't
write

return
to noise.

On Samoa Peninsula

Horizon
—left edge
a gray sliver
where the jetty
juts.

Notebook
propped up
by a stiff tuft
of beach grass.

You awake
within the poem.

The Dunes

A wave's wall
of foam

falls over
a night's

debris.
Starfish

dead in
splintered

driftwood
piled by

a spent
bonfire.

The panic
that would

pull me
under

somehow
recedes as

something's
shadow

clambers
from a tire-

flattened
tuft of

bush lupine.

Gold Bluffs

for Shannon Tharp

i.

Walls of moss
pliant
as the dark. Dark

crevices within, how
they hold and breathe

the salt-
coarsened air.

ii.

A stream
beneath
fallen alder

—roots
gnarled
over bolts

of lichen
attached
to stone.

iii.

What
sun's
left to
ribbon

rain

the moss-
cleaved
crags
absorb.

iv.

Lichen
scours
  the near-
black
  back to
what we
  forgot
was still
  day.

101

This revision
        of the hills

—sun sieved through low clouds
        and rain, the weight

given to green
        and clear-cut patches

—engulfs what I'm
        thinking,

or what you were
        saying.

And then an egret

        on the side of the road
nosing litter.

Elk Ridge

Night seeps
into its name.

At the edge
where black

oak clouds
an embankment

what I imagined
was silence

becomes enough
music for now—

the constellated
sounds

nouns

call out.

Won't Say

Rain reflecting
nothing
but rain. Stone

reflecting stone.
And litter,
litter; leaf, snail.

Sound heaped
on sound—
the imagined

intervals
mistaken
for breath

on the brink
of becoming
a word, *words*,

consumed
by what
syllables

won't say (*says it*)
while hydrangea
branches

bowed with water
knock the walls
into sleep.

December

after Barbara Guest

rust rust rust rust rust rust
only long rain long rain long
broad broad rain round rain numb

¤

Mock Orange

for John Coletti

i.

early spring's early agitation
—the dormant forms   this
                severed gestation

        —crow sounds assemble
a sustained syllable
open as the light   opening
                slit by slit
                around it

ii.

       sky's bound-
less articulation

        opens each
closed window

iii.

       lost a thought
while staring off
          into windows
across the street—

          traffic's reflection, the
glass in motion

iv.

over afternoon's slant

the haze swells, breaks

and gathers again
in staggered
sequence

above hills

v.

docks swallowed
        in fog—

a transient talks
        into a pine cone—

vi.

there in the brier
plastic bags
and torn clothing

    make the shade
    tangible

vii.

peripheral slippage
                    of leaves
white with sun
        submerging them

        follows me, follows
a dragonfly
        before dissolving

in the green reflection
                its thorax
        throws off

viii.

turn toward   the ocean—
what little's
visible   from here—
see the
gray glare,

                another
                front
                coming

ix.

               an otherwise un-
spoken space

                between door frame
and hedge

                made active
                    by gnats

¤

For a Last Page

Memory moves
forward and back-
ward—an echo
gathering more
and more silence.

Acknowledgments

Many of these poems were previously published in chapbooks: *Eureka Slough* (Effing Press), *The Lack Of* (Nasturtium Press), *Exit North* (Book Thug) and *Mock Orange* (Longhouse). Thanks to Scott Pierce, Claire Donato, Jay MillAr and Bob Arnold for their fine press work.

And some of these poems—often in alternate versions—appeared in journals and magazines: *BafterC*, *Burnside Review*, *The Cultural Society*, *Mary*, *A Public Space*, *Poets.org*, *Quarterly West*, *The Raleigh Quarterly*, *RealPoetik* and *Verse*.

"From a Window" appeared in the anthology *Visiting Dr. Williams: Poems Inspired by the Life and Work of William Carlos Williams* (University of Iowa Press).

The title "A Line Made by Walking" is from a work by Richard Long.

Thanks to Shannon Tharp, Andrew Mister, Anthony Robinson, Jess Mynes, Andrew Hughes, Pam Rehm, Zach Barocas, Steven Fama, Lily Brown, Richard Tacey, Scott Holmquist, Kathy Glass, Ashley Capps, Louise Mathias, John Coletti, Ryan Murphy, Steven Moore, Laura Sims and Floyd—for the camaraderie.

At the Point is Joseph Massey's second full-length collection. The first, *Areas of Fog*, was published in 2009 by Shearsman Books. All of the work contained in these books was written in Humboldt County, California, where he's lived for the last ten years.